THE Window BUILDER

· A MIRACLE FOR MOM ·

To Madison 2H

I hope you seek + find many miracles in your life.

T Johnson

THE Window BUILDER

A MIRACLE FOR MOM

KELLY HOOSE JOHNSON

SWEETWATER BOOKS
AN IMPRINT OF CEDAR FORT, INC.
SPRINGVILLE, UTAH

ISBN 13: 978-1-4621-1113-6

Published by Sweetwater Books, an imprint of Cedar Fort, Inc.
2373 W. 700 S., Springville, UT 84663
Distributed by Cedar Fort, Inc., www.cedarfort.com

LIBRARY OF CONGRESS CATALOGING-IN-PUBLICATION DATA

Johnson, Kelly Hoose, 1978- author.
  The window builder / Kelly Hoose Johnson.
    pages cm
  Summary: As a Christmas gift to his mother, sixteen-year-old Jason tries to replace a broken window with a stained glass replica of a Christmas ornament his parents had cherished.
  ISBN 978-1-4621-1113-8
  1. Christmas stories. I. Title.
  PS3610.O3593W56 2012
  813'.6--dc23
                                            2012027045

Cover design by Brian Halley
Cover design © 2012 by Lyle Mortimer
Edited and typeset by Whitney A. Lindsley

Printed in the United States of America

10 9 8 7 6 5 4 3 2 1

Printed on acid-free paper

For Lauryl—
the reasons innumerable

*T*INY FLECKS OF COLOR DANCED ACROSS THE wall as Jason held the stained glass up. It gave him a chill knowing his father had held this same ornament, had watched it spin and twirl in his hand.

Until a few years ago, it had always been the first ornament on the Christmas tree. Jason's mother would pull it out of the box while his father played "Pomp and Circumstance" on a pretend trumpet. She'd hang it carefully in front of a yellow light near the top. Then she'd turn to his father, and they'd laugh and laugh until they cried. Finally, wiping away the tears, his mother would say, "Okay, boys! Let the decorating commence!"

The reason they laughed about the ornament had

always been a mystery to Jason and his twin brother, Carter. He and Carter had asked what was so funny, but his father would raise an eyebrow, lower his voice, and say, "I'll tell you one day when you're older—or when you fall in love. Whichever comes first. And it had *better* be the first."

They could never get their parents to tell. But Jason still remembered how his mother's nose would wrinkle up when she laughed and how the lights from the Christmas tree cast merry colors across her face. He remembered the warmth of the fire and the smell of cinnamon rolls and butter. Those were happy Christmases.

He wanted that again this year.

It was a cold day. The morning sun, though bright through the window, didn't warm him. Jason angled the ornament toward and away from the sun, hypnotized by its intricate, glittering design. With every rotation of his wrist, new and vibrant splashes of light flashed across his room.

"Jason!" his mother called from the kitchen. "What's taking you so long? You'll be late for the bus!"

He stretched and checked his watch. He had at least three minutes. His mother always overreacted.

But stressing her out this morning was part of the plan. His mom was smart, and she had to be off routine not to suspect anything. He waited another minute before sitting up and swinging his legs over the edge of his top bunk. Just like every morning, the vibration from him jumping down shook the whole house.

The air smelled fantastic. His mother had made him and Carter breakfast for as long as he could remember. Now that she was in law school and working long hours as a paralegal, she didn't have the time. But somehow she still managed to cook for them one morning a week.

He had dressed and packed early today, but of course his mother didn't know that. He looked in the mirror and roughed up his hair to make it look like he'd thrown his hoodie on in a rush. Wrapping the ornament carefully in layers of tissue, he nestled it into a protected pocket inside his backpack. Slinging his bag onto his shoulder, he hurried into the kitchen and grabbed a piece of toast off his twin's plate.

"Hey!" Carter cried. "I was gonna eat that!"

Perfect, thought Jason. *Good job, Carter.*

"C'mon, Carter," Jason said. "Or we'll be late for the bus."

Carter grabbed his own backpack from under the table and followed him.

His mom's breakfasts were always great, but on a cold morning like this they were even better because all the warm food was accompanied by even warmer hot chocolate. The hardest part of staying in his room had been avoiding the breakfast table. His stomach was rumbling.

"Sorry, Mom," said Jason. "Had to finish some math homework." He ripped off a large piece of toast and managed an almost incomprehensible, "Big test today."

His mom, already in a skirt and high heels, raised an eyebrow but said nothing. She finished stuffing her satchel full of completed case studies before shooting a spatula across the room, basketball style. Jason watched it arc across the kitchen and land in the sink, splattering eggs across the backsplash.

"Boom!" she yelled. "Two points!"

He and Carter both laughed as they headed for the door.

"Oh, hey, I almost forgot!" Jason turned, holding open the screen door as Carter pushed past, running through the yard to stop the bus which was just pulling away. "I'm tutoring some sophomores this afternoon, integrated engineering track. I'll be home late."

"Do you want me to pick you up after I'm finished at work?" his mom asked.

"Nah, I'll walk or find a ride. It's not supposed to snow until way late tonight." He turned again, not giving her a chance to respond, and called over his shoulder, "Love you!" before bolting for the bus. Carter was hanging halfway out the door to keep the bus driver from driving off without him.

"Thanks for waiting," Jason said to the red-haired woman as he climbed aboard.

She smirked. "Thank your twin."

When they settled into their seat, Carter slid a large lump of aluminum foil from his backpack, chock-full of cold scrambled eggs and bacon.

"No way!" said Jason before digging in with his fingers.

"I know you think you're clever," Carter said, "but I get the prize this morning. Do you know how hard it is to sneak a meal out from under Mom's nose?"

"I hope you were *really* sneaky. She can't be suspicious of anything, no matter how small."

"Please." Carter gave him a withering look. "How could you doubt me? I'm offended. Besides, I think you're over-planning, like always. Mom's not going to suspect the classified details of your scheme just because you're a little later than usual coming home."

"Maybe. But I'd rather be sneaky than make her worry about why I'm home late. I hate it when she worries."

After he shoveled in the last of his eggs, Jason leaned his head back on the cold leather seat and said, "Mom's the best. I really hope this cheers her up."

"Okay. Speaking of Mom," Carter said. "You've thought this plan right up through getting the new window made. If that actually works—*if* that actually works, how exactly do you expect to install it without her noticing?"

"Well, the busted window is already covered in cardboard. If we can get her out of the house long enough—an hour or two maybe—I'll put in the new window and cover it back up, exactly the way it was. She'll think it's still broken on Christmas morning and then—voilà!—a beautiful stained glass replacement."

Carter cocked his head and stared out the window as if he wasn't listening. Jason understood. It meant he was thinking.

"My first preseason basketball scrimmage is next week," said Carter. "If you can have it ready by then, I'll be certain she comes to cheer me on."

Perfect. Mom would never miss a basketball game. Carter, maybe you're *the best*, Jason thought.

Out loud he said, "Don't stink it up so she comes home early."

After school, Jason skipped Architecture Club and got a ride with his best friend, Madison, to a house just outside of town. Madison was in the integrated engineering track too, and if anyone could help him design and install a new window, she could. She was perky and always wore something bright pink, whether it went with the rest of her outfit or not. Today it was neon-pink, knee-high socks. Pulled up, they almost met her camouflage skirt. A stripe of white in her dark hair completed the picture.

". . . and I'm absolutely positive you will love this guy. It's not just his artistry or his technology or his skills. It's his demeanor. It's his character. He's so . . . so . . ." She had been talking about Philip Fitzsimmons, The Window Builder, nonstop since they pulled out of the school parking lot, but with a sigh, her words failed her for once.

"Amazing?" Jason tried.

"So much more than amazing," she replied. "You'll see. He'll change your life."

A gravel road took them through a cornfield to Philip's house. It wasn't late when they arrived, but with the time change, the sun was already setting. Jason stepped out of the car and looked up at the harvested rows of cornstalks, empty and brittle. The wind blew, rustling the leaves. He shivered. He wasn't sure if it was the wind or the strange feeling he had about this place.

Philip's house was small, the exterior painted the same yellow as the corn. No wonder you couldn't see it from the main road. Two rocking chairs were placed on the porch on either side of the front door.

The windows on the house were sparkling clean, but other than that, they were ordinary. A rusted sign hooked over the porch railing read "The Window Builder" with an arrow that pointed to the right.

Madison led the way around the house, down a narrow footpath through the stalks. They walked for several minutes before stepping into a gravel-strewn clearing with a low gray barn at its center. The doors were open at both ends, and Jason could see straight through the barn to the cornfield on the other side.

Although dusk was falling around him, the inside of the barn was so brightly lit that Jason felt as if he were in a dream, a sharp image in the center of fading edges. Individual stalls ran down each side of the barn, but it wasn't obvious what was inside them.

Staring down the middle, Jason noticed the barn was empty except for a large glass desk that was lined from one side to the other with what appeared to be high-definition computer monitors, also made of glass. A man sat in front of the monitors, manipulating 3-D images on every screen in quick succession—mixing, matching, and overlaying schematics.

"Whoa," Jason said. "That's a sweet setup. Are you sure we don't need an appointment?" The man—Philip, Jason assumed—concentrated on his work. Jason could only see the back of his head, but it didn't look like he would welcome an interruption.

"Don't be silly. If we needed an appointment, I'd have made an appointment," Madison replied. "Philip," she called out. "I have a new client for you!"

Philip raised his head and, without turning around, said, "Madison."

To Jason's surprise, Madison clutched his arm. He looked down at her. Her eyes were shining. She whispered, "He remembers me."

Philip turned now to gaze at her, a wide smile on his face. Despite a full auburn beard, Jason could see every straight white tooth. His matching auburn hair, flecked with gray, was mussed in a way Jason wished he could replicate. There was no doubt about it—for an older man working alone in a barn, he was stylish. And strong. It was hard for Jason to ignore the width of his shoulders.

Before Jason could fully size him up, Philip

sprang to his feet and opened his arms. Madison rushed to him, and he lifted her off her feet. He spun her in a circle, both of them laughing.

Jason's jaw dropped.

Philip gave Jason a quick wink before setting Madison back on her feet. He bustled to retrieve a couple of folding chairs placed against a stall and opened them so they formed a little circle with his own. Madison sat right down. Philip motioned for Jason to join them.

Jason shuffled in and took a seat. He felt out of place, like he was interrupting a family reunion. He took a deep breath and prepared to introduce himself with a mere handshake, but before he could begin, Philip leaned toward Madison and gazed intently into her face.

"How's Taliatha?" he asked.

Madison bit her lip and a small crease formed between her eyebrows. "She's . . . safe," she answered.

Philip stroked his beard and nodded. His eyes shifted, staring into the descending darkness outside the barn. Jason looked from one to the other. He had no idea what they were talking about, and once again he felt like an intruder.

"Philip," Madison said, coming to the rescue, "This is one of my best friends, Jason. He needs your help."

"Ah!" Philip exclaimed, extending his hand as if he had just noticed Jason for the first time. "Welcome to the barn. I assume you've come for a window."

As they shook hands, Jason felt warmth start in his hand and tingle up his arm. It stopped as soon as they let go, right above his elbow.

Philip waved a finger at Jason. "But not an ordinary window—am I right?

Jason nodded his head, overtaken by Philip's larger-than-life personality.

"Tell me what you're looking for," said Philip.

Jason slipped his bag off his shoulder and positioned it at his feet. He was still staring at his own arm as he pulled out the tissue and unwrapped the ornament. *What had caused that tingling?*

Jason held up the stained glass, and Philip let out a low whistle.

"Now that's a beauty," he said. "Where did you get it?"

"I don't know exactly. Somewhere in Europe, I think. All I know for sure is that my dad bought it for my mom a long time ago and that it's been the first ornament we've hung on our Christmas tree every year since," he replied.

"May I examine it?" Philip asked.

"Sure," Jason said, handing it over.

Philip held it up and tipped his head back, looking down his nose to view it as it dangled and twirled above him. His face was awash in lively streaks of color as the bright lights from the barn illuminated his face through the stained glass. His mouth parted, and his eyes moved rapidly, taking in the details.

"Hm . . . five-inch circular. It's a sophisticated pattern, probably based off the window of an old castle or cathedral." He ran his finger around the outer edge. "Real ironwork," he said, eyebrows raised. "You say it's been on the tree every Christmas? So that would make it, what? About sixteen or seventeen years old?"

"Well, almost every Christmas," Jason said, correcting himself.

"I see." Philip returned the ornament. "It's a nice piece. No flaws that I can see. What do you want me to do with it?"

"I want to make a replica, only bigger, to fit a broken window in my mom's bedroom. Some neighbor kids accidently broke it a while ago, and she hasn't had it fixed yet. I'm not sure why. Time, maybe. Or maybe money."

He looked at Madison, feeling embarrassed. She knew his story, but it was still a little awkward talking about money out loud. Her life wasn't perfect, but she definitely had money.

"I've been saving all year for this. So has my twin brother. We think we have enough."

"Stained glass windows can be pretty expensive," Philip replied. He pursed his lips a moment before saying, "But there are some options that could reduce the price. What else can you tell me?"

Jason rushed the rest; he'd been thinking about it a long time.

"See, the window faces east, so it will light up beautifully as the sun rises. And my mom's always up early to get ready for the day. The ornament made her happy when my dad was alive. But the last few years she's been so sad at Christmastime, and when I tried to hang it up last year, she took it from me and stuffed it in a drawer. I think, maybe, if my brother and I can give this to her ourselves, and she sees it every day, and she knows how much we love her, she'll know it's okay to put it on the tree again."

After listening intently, Philip said, "Let's work up the dimensions."

They hovered around the monitors as Philip did a rough mock-up. In half an hour, the three of them had figured out most of the engineering details.

"Okay, come with me," Philip said. "I'll give you some glass samples. Each one has a different price and will have a different look when it's hung. Take them home and test them in the morning light. Call me when you've decided, and I'll give you the bottom line for the whole window."

Jason let out a deep breath. He hoped this would work.

Philip led them into one of the stalls.

"This is your least expensive option," he said, waving his hand across rows and rows of slot cabinets. Hundreds of sheets of glass sat in them, organized by color. "It's imported, and once I cut the pieces and put them in place, the window is finished." He nabbed a broken piece of blue glass from a bucket to one side, about palm sized. "Don't forget. This is the one that's imported."

Jason swallowed hard. *Imported* sounded expensive, and this was the cheapest of the three options.

They moved to a second stall. This one had a project laid out on a long table. The stained glass depicted a dense tropical forest with an ocean in the background. The entire scene was edged with leaves and ruby-colored fruits. The work was exquisite.

"See how the glass has texture?" Philip motioned to the surface and let Jason and Madison run their fingers over it. "I can glue special pieces to the base layer so it appears chipped, rounded, jeweled—any effect you want." Philip reached into another bucket at his feet, and grabbed a green cast-off. The faceting made it look like a slender slip of emeralds.

"This is my favorite type of work, but it's time-consuming, so it's pricier." He handed the piece to Jason, who held it to the light in awe as they walked from the second stall into a third.

"Now if it's authenticity you're going for, this is the best choice." This time the artwork was braced against the back wall. Half the pieces were clear, and the other half had been painted.

"I've just started this one, but I think you'll see how detailed it is when you compare it to the original picture." Philip handed them a photo of a little girl standing beside a fawn. So far Philip's replication was exact.

Philip reached over and flipped a switch, lighting up a panel behind the glass. Then he took a remote control from his pocket, chuckled, and said, "Watch this."

He pushed a button, and all the lights in the barn went out except for the light behind the panel. The effect was startling. Jason saw every nuance of the deer as though it was trembling, about to leap off the glass.

The barn lights came back on, and Philip explained. "I paint this with powdered glass." He gestured to some vials sitting on a stool. "It's an extremely fine powder. I can mix the colors with water to create any shade I want. Then I fire the finished pieces with a hand-torch. You've seen the results for yourself. If you want, I can make your new window look exactly like your mom's ornament in every way, but it is the most expensive of the three options."

He reached into a third bucket and rummaged for a while before extracting a piece painted with a delicate pink flower. It was shaded so perfectly that Jason's first reaction was to smell it.

"I think three samples will do, don't you?" He looked at Madison with a twinkle in his eye. She grinned then nodded.

"Excuse me while I wrap these for you. And . . . oh!" Philip snapped his fingers. "Can I scan your ornament too?" Jason handed all four pieces to Philip.

He headed back toward his desk, calling over his shoulder, "Feel free to look around for a few minutes."

Jason and Madison moved from stall to stall, examining Philip's handiwork. It wasn't all stained glass. He had created stunning blown-glass sculptures, large and small. One entire stall was dedicated to handmade glass jewelry. Madison was especially fascinated by these pieces. Intricate, delicate, simple, vintage—it was a broad collection. She tried on several necklaces before they moved to the next area. It contained utilitarian items like glass plates, vases, and cups. There were even a few industrial projects in the barn, like oversized panes he was rolling with shatterproof film.

When they were finished, they wandered back to Philip's desk. He was already busy formulating a new project on his monitors.

"Thanks for everything," Jason said.

Philip nodded. "Call me as soon as you've decided." He handed Jason his business card then winked at Madison, who broke out in a brilliant smile.

By the time Madison dropped Jason off, snow was falling from the sky in heavy swirls. On the drive home, the headlights lit up every flake, cutting two beams of constant motion before them. Madison had been uncharacteristically quiet. Jason had tried starting up a conversation by asking who Taliatha was, but she shook her head, smiled, and said, "It's personal."

Jason wondered how personal it could be if she had told Philip, but he decided not to push it and let Madison concentrate on the road.

Madison pulled up in front of Jason's house. Jason climbed out, his skin smarting in the cold. From the curb, he leaned back into the car and said, "Drive safely."

"Don't worry. I will."

"Really, though. Be careful. Watch for ice, okay?"

Jason knew his warnings could be annoying, but he couldn't help himself. His dad had died in a car accident on an icy day.

Madison bit her lip. She sucked in a quick breath and opened her mouth to say something. Jason leaned in further. But she changed her mind and simply said, "Thanks. I'll be extra careful."

He waved as she drove away, thinking about all that had happened that evening. He was home much later than he had planned. He hoped all his creative secrecy this morning had paid off and his mother wasn't sitting inside worrying.

$\mathcal{T}$HE NEXT MORNING, JASON CLIMBED OUT OF bed before sunrise, careful not to jump and shake the house when he landed. Carter, asleep in the bottom bunk, heard him anyway. He cracked an eye and asked him where he was going.

"Outside," Jason whispered. "Got to see what I can see by the dawn's early light."

Carter snickered and then rolled over and went back to sleep.

Jason knew his mother would be up and had possibly already been up for hours doing homework. He cracked his door and peeked out toward her room. Her light was on, but lucky for him, her bedroom door was closed. He crept to the front door, stopping only to throw his coat and boots on over his pajamas.

Once outside, he unwrapped the first sample—the blue glass—and stuffed the others in his coat pocket. Daybreak came slowly. He passed the time shivering and making puffs of cloud with his breath. As the sun began to crest, he held the glass up to the eastern horizon. It was sharp at the edges, and he had to pinch it gingerly not to cut himself.

As the least ornate of the three samples, he didn't expect to gaze at it long, but he needed a proper comparison. He glanced through the glass and saw some movement on the other side.

Jason laughed out loud.

What in the world? I should get up early more often.

Two of his neighbors were out in the snow, dancing. He dropped his arm to get a better look.

They were gone.

He checked in all directions. How could they have moved so quickly?

Okay . . . that was weird.

Jason raised his arm again, and the moment he gazed at the glass, his neighbors were back.

He dropped his arm a second time, and a second time they disappeared.

Not. Possible.

Slowly he raised the glass to his face and peered

through it carefully. He shook his head in disbelief. The image was *inside* the glass. He lowered it again, perplexed.

But when he looked another time, it was obvious. There were two people, seemingly inside the glass. He squinted and made out their forms. They were distant, and because of the tint of the glass, they were blue.

He held the glass up directly to the sun, and the whole image changed. In an eddy of light, the people twirled nearer and nearer. They changed color too, became more solid. The man wore a red scarf. The woman wore a pink hat and mittens. As they wheeled together, Jason's breath caught in his chest and his mouth dropped open.

The people were his parents.

Only they were young. The image played like an old film, the periphery hazy and blue. Now he could see buildings in the background. He squinted again— Dartmouth College. He knew it from pictures. It was where his parents had met and fallen in love.

And now he was watching them. So young. Dancing in the snow.

Jason closed his eyes tight. When he opened them, his parents were still there.

He sat down in the snow and stared at the glass,

mesmerized. The snow soaked him, but he didn't care. He braced his elbows on his knees, holding the glass to the sun, and kept watching.

Abruptly, the scene changed.

His parents were now in class together, holding hands under the desk.

The glass changed again. This time he saw his father kneel in the snow by a frozen pond, proposing to his mother. She dropped to her knees, cupped his face in her hands, and kissed him. Deeply.

Jason felt his face flush before the glass changed a fourth time. This time his parents stood before a justice of the peace—his father in a suit, his mother in a white dress—with friends seated on both sides.

He watched as they boarded a giant jet, snuggling together between two other passengers. The scene lasted a long time, and nothing happened except that his mother finally fell asleep, but Jason had no desire to look away. He watched his mother, her face serene, her head resting on his father's shoulder. It had been a long time since he had seen her so free from worry.

Finally the jet landed, and he watched them deplane. He got a single glance of the Eiffel Tower before the image changed again, looping back to the scene of them dancing in the snow.

Jason watched the reel again until a car drove

down the street and broke his concentration. It slowed significantly as it passed him. He realized he must have looked ridiculous sitting in the snow in a coat and pajamas and staring at the sun through a piece of blue glass. Absorbed in what he had been viewing, he hadn't appreciated his legs were numb too. He had just begun to stretch them when the front door clattered open.

"Jason!" his mother called. "*What* are you *doing* out here?"

He stuffed the glass into his pocket, pricking a finger in his haste. He suppressed a grimace and wracked his brain for an appropriate response.

"Madison and I made a bet. She said I couldn't sit in the snow for longer than five minutes. I told her I could." He felt bad about lying to his mom. He'd been doing it a lot lately.

"What?"

She wasn't convinced.

"Is that what you two were arguing about?" Carter peeked around his mother's shoulders. "You're ridiculous." He grinned. "So, what did you bet?"

Jason's eyes grew wide. "We bet, uh . . ."

"Whatever," Carter cut him off. "Hey! Take off your boots! Let's see who can stand barefoot in the snow longer. I'll bet you a week of chores I win."

"You're on!" Jason said, hoping his mother would buy it.

Carter tiptoed out barefoot as Jason flung off his boots.

She threw up her hands. "Don't stand out there all morning, you two. I don't care if you both get frostbite—you will still do your chores." She put on her dress coat and pulled her keys out of her purse. "I'm off to work." She pointed at them with two fingers as she treaded cautiously down the icy sidewalk in her high heels. "*Don't* miss the bus. *Do* eat some breakfast. And *don't* be home late." She shot them a saccharine smile. "*Do* remember that I love you."

She almost slipped but reached the car just in time to catch herself. The boys laughed. She glowered back and said, "Laughing at me? You're the monkeys standing barefoot in the snow."

She climbed in and backed slowly down the driveway. As she pulled away, she rolled down the window, and yelled out, "I really do love you!"

Jason and Carter waved as she drove away. Then Carter cursed and ran inside. Jason grabbed his boots and followed him.

"Does this mean I win?" Jason asked, stamping his feet on the carpet.

"You wish! I win for saving your bacon. Mom

didn't believe a word you said until I intervened." Carter curled up on the couch and rubbed his feet. "So, did you pick one?"

Jason sobered. "Carter, you've *got* to see something. Put on your boots."

"No way! Whatever piece you picked, I believe it's the right choice. My feet are not going back outside until they've thawed."

"I'm serious, Carter. There's something you have to see. And you can only see it in the right light."

Carter grumbled, but he got up and snatched his boots from their spot by the front door. As they sat to fasten them, for spite, Carter put his bare toes on the back of Jason's neck.

"Ugh! Knock it off!" Jason yelled.

"Just sayin'," Carter replied. "This had better be worth it."

Back in the snow, Jason gave his brother the blue glass. "You have to hold it so the sun shines right through."

"Well, yeah. It's stained glass," Carter replied. He held it up for a moment then nodded. "Nice," he said, handing it back.

Jason rubbed his eyebrow with the back of his hand. "Did you see anything unusual? No? Try looking more closely."

"Okaaaay . . ." Carter moved the piece closer to his face and tipped his head. He squinted. He squinted harder.

Yes, thought Jason. *That's it. Now you're seeing it.*

"I don't get it," Carter said. "What do you want me to notice? Because obviously you're the expert, not me."

"You didn't see . . . Mom and Dad?"

"Ummm . . . no." Carter gave Jason a placating pat on the shoulder before placing the glass back in his hand. "I know you've been planning this project for a long time, but methinks you're taking it too seriously. I'm gonna go get breakfast now."

Jason stared at his brother's back, dumbfounded. He held the glass to the sun, and there they were, as clear as ever—his parents dancing in the snow.

"Did you know?" Jason's question sounded more like an accusation.

Madison closed her locker and lowered her eyes. "Of course I knew." She looked up at him. "Why did you think I was so excited for you?"

"So it's real then?"

"I don't know what you saw. But yes, it's real.

And I don't know how he does it, but Philip builds very special windows."

"Taliatha," Jason said, remembering. "That's why you talked about her. That's how he knew."

"Yes."

"Who was she? Why is she safe? Why is that important to you?"

"That doesn't matter now. Do you want to talk about it? I'm the only one who'll believe you. And you're the only one who can see what you saw. Trust me. I tried to share my 'visions' with other people. They thought I was crazy." Madison snorted. "At first so did I. But whatever you saw, it's a gift. He's giving you a gift."

"All I *wanted* was a stained glass window."

Jason didn't know why he felt angry. Madison was right. He had loved watching his parents dance. He felt like he knew too much and too little, all at the same time.

They started walking to their next class.

"Did you examine all three pieces?" she asked.

"No, I didn't have time."

"You need to look at all of them, as soon as possible. Skip class. I'll cover for you in chemistry."

"I can't . . ."

"Yes, you can." Madison said. She pulled him

into the open door of an empty classroom. "This is really important, Jason. Do you still have the card Philip gave you? Take it out."

Jason hadn't taken the time to read it last night. He had jammed it in his wallet.

Now they both held Philip's cards in their hands.

"They're identical," Jason said. "Name. Description. Phone number. Seems pretty normal to me."

"Flip it over," Madison said.

They both flipped their cards over.

Madison read hers first. "'*When Jason needs my services, call me.*' I know it sounds stupid, but after my experience, I *knew* you would ask me about a window one day. I *knew* it. What's yours say?"

Jason didn't want to know.

Madison read it to herself then held it in front of his eyes, so he couldn't avoid it.

When Carter needs my services, call me.

Jason felt the warmth in his arm again, the same way he did when he shook Philip's hand, tingling from his fingers to just above his elbow.

"What's happening, Madison? This can't be possible." His voice carried a plaintive tone.

"I don't—can't—understand it. But Philip did more for me than you know. Maybe I'll tell you, but right now, you need to look at the other samples."

Jason stared over her head for a long time.

"Okay," he said. "But give Mr. Mullen a reasonable story for my absence. And take good notes."

Madison grinned. "Believe in the impossible," she replied.

She popped onto her toes and gave him a peck on the cheek before running down the hall at the sound of the bell. She waved at the door and ducked into the classroom.

Jason rubbed his cheek and smiled. What a bizarre day.

This time Jason felt more prepared. He borrowed a blanket from the theater department and walked to a nearby park. He picked a spot facing the sun but sheltered from people. He snugged the blanket around himself and sat under a modern-art sculpture he had never understood. It had protected the ground from snowfall, so his pants stayed dry.

He pulled out the second sample, the green glass with contouring.

Jason breathed deeply—once, twice, three times—and held the glass to the light.

The scene came into focus.

His parents held hands and strolled around an old

cathedral somewhere in Paris, the Eiffel Tower still in the background. His father whispered something in his mother's ear before wandering off, counting a few French francs he had pulled from his pocket. Jason couldn't see his father, but his mother sat on a wall to wait for him.

Another man sidled up, and suddenly, Jason could hear them talking. But not with his ears. It was as if their conversation was happening inside his head.

"You are alone?" the man asked with a thick French accent.

"No," his mother answered. "My husband is here. Nearby."

"Ah, then. You do not want a boyfriend? Because I will be your boyfriend."

His mother laughed. "No, thank you. I would like you to leave."

"Are you very sure? I do not see your husband. Perhaps he is not coming back."

"My husband is right over there." She pointed off the glass. "I can see him. He's the tall one in the gray coat."

"Ah, then," said the Frenchman. "I am better looking. Perhaps you should choose me instead."

"You are *not* better looking! You can't even see his face!"

"No matter, I will love you better."

Jason's mother laughed and reached for something. His father walked back into the scene and handed her a baguette.

"James," she said. "This man would like to be my boyfriend."

"I see," his father answered. "What do you think? Should we interview him for the position?"

"I don't see why not," she replied.

The sensible thing would have been to ignore him. Instead they bombarded him with ridiculous questions. Where did he live? Would he relocate? Did he cook? Could he also cook crepes? What did he know of Descartes? Did he bathe daily? Could he get them tickets to Paris Fashion Week?

Their questions grew ever more preposterous. Was he a good handyman? Could he fix broken pipes? If there was a plague, could he play a pipe to lead the rats away?

It went on and on.

The passionate Frenchman had a response for everything, making it all the funnier. Jason found himself laughing out loud as his mom and dad took turns.

The poor would-be suitor never had a chance. Jason's parents hooted so hard at each new question that eventually his father snorted. This only made them laugh harder until his mother wiped the tears from her eyes. The Frenchman finally walked away, throwing a haughty retort over his shoulder, "You missed your chance, beautiful woman! Your boyfriend is leaving. And if you did not know, I am funnier than your gray-coated man too!"

His parents were in hysterics, stamping their feet and howling in laughter.

That's when Jason saw it. Above their heads, the cathedral in the background had a perfect stained glass window. It matched the ornament in his pocket exactly.

The scene changed.

Jason knew this image. It was his old house, the one they lived in before his father died.

A large Christmas tree stood in the bay window. His mother attempted to string it with lights, but she was heavily pregnant and couldn't reach some of the branches. Jason stared at her belly. He knew there had been two babies inside her, but he hadn't realized that she had ever grown that big.

His father snuck up behind her and whispered in her ear. She turned to him with a giant smile. Jason remembered that smile. It was the special smile that only his dad could coax from her. It had been too long since he had seen it.

"Trade you," his father said. He took the string of lights from her and placed a gift in her hand.

Her eyes glistened as she opened it. Inside the wrapping was a white box, and from the white box his mother drew out an ornament—an exquisite stained glass ornament.

"Oh, James," she said. "It's beautiful. From Paris, right?"

In answer, his father took it from her hand, held it between their faces, and said in a heavy French accent, "I will be . . . your boyfriend."

She burst into laughter, and her nose wrinkled up. His father helped her string the rest of the lights on the tree and then played "Pomp and Circumstance" on a pretend trumpet as he hung the ornament by a yellow light. They had no other ornaments that year.

The glass went blank. Jason blinked as pure sunlight streamed through. It seemed to gather inside him, warming his heart.

He finally knew. The ornament had always been their secret story. And now it was his too.

Jason wrapped the second shard and placed it in his pocket. He sat for almost an hour in the cold, quietly observing the park before pulling out his phone and dialing.

It rang once, twice, three times. Madison was probably making up an excuse to get out of class as she felt the phone buzzing in her pocket.

Four times. Five times. One more ring and it would go to voicemail.

"You okay?" She asked in a whisper.

It broke his concentration. "Why are you whispering?"

"We were in the middle of a lab experiment. I'm hiding in the chemical closet."

"Seriously? You're not supposed to be in the . . ."

"The closet of Enter-And-Be-Expelled? Yes, I know. Talk fast."

"Okay. I already asked, but who's Taliatha?"

Silence.

Jason didn't know if the silence was to avoid Mr. Mullen's wrath or if she didn't want to tell him.

He spoke again.

"I'm sorry. It's none of my business. You don't have to answer. It's just this whole magical—whatever— that's happening inside the glass. It seems genuine, and yet I don't know why I'm seeing it or what to make of it. I thought if you told me more about your experience with Philip, I could figure out if . . ."

"She's my sister."

"Your . . . what?" Jason thought she was an only child.

Madison blew out a deep breath. Through the cell phone it hurt Jason's ear.

"My birth mom had more children. One of them, Taliatha, was in trouble. It's complicated."

"I thought you didn't know who your birth mom was."

"I do now."

"Whoa."

"Yeah," Madison said. "Whoa. What you witness in the glass may be difficult. Somehow though, it will be perfect for you. I know it."

There was silence again as Jason let her words sink in.

"How did you find Philip?" he asked.

"Philip gave my aunt and uncle a business card with my name on the back. And *they* found him through a friend who received a business card with their names on the back. From what I can tell, that's the only way. The Window Builder isn't exactly in the phone book."

"You've kept a lot to yourself."

"Yes, I have. Listen, I need to go. Call me later?"

"I will. Don't get caught."

Jason readjusted to the sun and pulled out the third glass sample—the piece with the delicate pink flower.

He held it to the light, and when the scene became clear, for the first time, he saw himself.

He and Carter were eating breakfast at the kitchen table in their old house, their bigger house. It was only a few years ago, but they had both grown a lot since then.

The house was decorated for Christmas. Garland wound around the staircase. Cookies sat on a poinsettia-shaped plate on the kitchen table. Their Christmas tree stood tall in the background. Although the tree was partially obstructed by an arch, Jason could see the stained glass ornament at the top, twinkling in the morning light.

His mother was in the kitchen. She looked gloomy. She threw food into the refrigerator like she didn't care where it landed. A carton of eggs didn't quite make the shelf and tipped over. She snatched at the eggs in vain before they smashed on the floor in a messy, slimy pile.

Jason put the glass down.

Not that day. Please, no. Not that day.

Of everything he could show him, why would Philip make him watch this day?

It was the day his father died, only a couple of weeks before Christmas.

Jason knew. He remembered the day started with broken eggs.

He didn't want to look into the glass, but he heard Madison's voice in his head. *He's giving you a gift. What you witness in the glass may be difficult. Somehow though, it will be perfect for you. I know it.*

Jason steeled himself and held the stained glass up toward the sun again.

He watched his mother clean up the eggs while he and Carter continued to eat.

Don't be stupid, he thought. *Get up and help her!*

But he knew he hadn't helped and nothing could change the past. His mother packed a couple of brown bag lunches and gave him and Carter kisses as they rushed out the door. They didn't kiss her back. They didn't even look back. They just ran away.

She closed the door behind them and began to cry.

She cried while she cleaned their plates off the table and cried while she put the milk away.

Jason felt helpless.

His father walked out of their bedroom. He finished knotting his tie then joined his mother at the sink, rinsing dishes and placing them in the dishwasher. He looked uncomfortable, like he didn't know what to say. They worked side by side for a while, neither of them speaking or looking at each other. His mother was still sniffling.

"Charlene," he said. "I know it hurts, but it's okay."

"It is *not* okay," she said, slamming the sponge down on the edge of the sink.

His father held up both hands like he was surrendering. "I know. But it will be okay. In the future. Another day."

"After all these years!" She was crying in full force again. "A miscarriage? It's not okay today, and it will never be okay! James, I really wanted this baby."

Jason was shocked. Had she said *a miscarriage*?

Not only had he almost had another sibling, but his mother—she must have lost two family members in the same week.

The scene continued.

His father dried his hands, then moved to the family room and sat on the couch. He invited her to sit next to him, but she refused. When he didn't respond, she got angry.

"Nothing to say?" she demanded. "The silence isn't helping."

"I don't know what you want from me." His tone was heavy.

"I want your support!"

"I'm trying, but I don't know what to say. I don't know how to help. I think what you need is some time."

"Time?" She was shouting now. "What I need is *time*? I need my baby back!"

She burst into tears again. He went to her, tried to give her a hug, but she shrugged him off.

"Just go to work!" she shouted. "Come back when you can be helpful!"

He opened his mouth, but no words came out. He tipped his head back and stared at the ceiling.

"All right," he said. "If that's what you want."

"Yes," she said, sounding even more annoyed that he had agreed.

"Fine," he replied, walking to the front door. "You know how to reach me . . . if you need anything."

She said nothing.

He put on his suit coat, scarf, and gloves and reached for the knob. He hesitated before trying one more time. "Can I still be your boyfriend?"

Her angry eyes turned to slits as she turned her back on him.

The scene changed again, and Jason assumed it would be his father's funeral. But it wasn't. It was his father, coming in the front door, still dressed in his suit. How was this possible? His father had died in a car accident in the middle of the day. How could he be home?

His father checked his watch then sat at the kitchen table and pulled out a sheet of paper and a pen. The view changed. Jason saw the paper, as if he were his father, saw what he was writing as he scrawled each letter on the page.

Dearest Charlene,

The first thing I admit is that I don't know how you feel. You loved that baby. You wanted it more than anything. I'm a good man, and I wanted that baby too. But I'm not you, and I don't know what it has been like for you. If I did, I would know what to say and how to act and how to love you best. Until then, I hope you can be patient with me. I'll keep trying.

You are an amazing woman. You're a great mother to Jason and Carter. It can't be easy living with three men, but you love us and laugh with us and are so strong. I know that whatever happens, you will always be strong.

I'm guessing that right about now, you're cheering Carter on at his basketball game, feeling guilty about our fight this morning. I know you, and I bet you feel terrible for shouting at me. I'll be honest—I don't think I deserved it. But I don't mind. It's over now. I love you too much to stay upset. So when you get this note, please understand that when I come home, all I want is to hold you tight. No regrets.

If I think of the right thing to do, I'll do it. If I think of the right words, I'll say them. But until then, remember I love you. I'll always love you, no matter what.

Your forever boyfriend,

James

He folded the paper over and left it in the middle of the kitchen table. Then he thought better of it.

"Flowers," he muttered. "It would be better with flowers."

Jason watched his father hide the letter on top of some built-in shelves in the living room. He slid it into a one-inch gap between the top shelf and the ceiling. Then he walked out the front door, and the glass went blank.

A LETTER.

His father had written a letter to his mother before going out for flowers. But there weren't flowers in the car when he died. The accident must have happened on his way to the flower shop. And his mother had never gotten the letter because he had hidden it.

That must be why she hid the ornament, why she had never moved on from his death. They had fought. She had turned her back on him. And she had never forgiven herself for that ending.

Jason called Madison again.

"Can you pick me up? I'm at Lincoln Park."

"I'll be there in three minutes," she said.

Three minutes later, Jason hopped in the car.

"Take me to my old house?"

"On our way."

Madison didn't ask any questions until they arrived. "Want me to go with you?"

Jason considered saying yes then changed his mind. "No. It's okay."

He knocked on the door. He didn't know the new owners, and he wasn't sure how to explain. An elderly woman with white hair opened the door.

"May I help you?"

"I hope the answer is yes. I used to live here, and I just found out there's a document that my mom really needs that's still in the house. Would you mind if I came in and looked?"

"Oh, I assure you, young man, we've cleaned out all the drawers."

"It wasn't in a drawer, ma'am. I would really like to find it. Would you please let me in?"

She became distressed and called to her husband.

Jason explained himself a second time, telling the man that the document he needed was on top of the built-in bookcase in the living room.

"I guess you can come in," he said eventually. "But I've got my cell phone right here in my hand. I'm dialing 911, and if you try anything at all, I'm going to push send."

Normally Jason would have laughed, but he was too relieved to find it funny.

"Thank you! Can I borrow a chair?"

The old man nodded.

Jason climbed up and slid his hand into the tiny space between the shelf and the ceiling, exactly where he'd seen his father place the letter. He didn't feel anything. He swept his hand back and forth, but all he swept out was dust. He climbed from the chair onto a higher shelf, ignoring the sharp inhale from the old woman behind him.

He peered into the crack.

There it was!

At the back of the bookcase, right against the wall was a folded piece of paper. There was no way he could reach it with his hand.

"I can see it!" he called. "Do you have something thin and long, so I can reach it?"

The old man shuffled in another room for a long time and eventually procured a yardstick. Jason pulled the paper toward him. He breathed a sigh of relief and climbed down.

Jason's hands shook as he opened it.

It was his father's writing. It was *the* letter.

"Thank you," he whispered to the old couple, his eyes filling with tears.

The woman cocked her head. "Are you all right?"

"Yes," Jason said. "Yes, I am. Thank you again. I'll leave now."

The man hung up the phone and walked him to the front door. "Anything else I should know about that you'll be hunting for someday?"

Jason laughed. "I don't know, sir. I hope not."

When Jason climbed back into Madison's car, he was drying his eyes. He couldn't hide it, but he wasn't ashamed. He was grateful—grateful to his father, his mother, Carter, Madison, and especially to Philip.

"Where to now?" Madison asked.

"Let's go see Philip," Jason answered.

Madison grinned. "Yes, sir." She spun the wheel and did a U-turn toward the main road out of town. "Have you ever skipped class before today?" she asked.

"Never," he said. "I even try to come to school when I'm sick. My mom stops me."

"Ew, yuck. Good for your mom."

"I'd ask if you've ever skipped class, but I already know the answer."

Madison snickered. "So, what's that in your hand?"

"I'll tell you in a minute." Jason pulled out his phone and fumbled through his wallet for Philip's business card. "I've got to thank him first."

His call went straight to voicemail.

"You've reached Philip Fitzsimmons, *The Window Builder.* Every client is important. Leave a message. I'll help if I can."

"Philip, I found it! I found the letter! My mother will be so . . . so . . . I don't even know what to say. I'm calling to thank you for . . ."

Jason's phone buzzed.

". . . for . . ."

It buzzed again. Someone else was calling. He looked at the number and answered.

"Philip?"

"Jason!" It was Philip's voice. "I'm so glad you called! I was busy with another very important client, but I wanted to know which glass sample you liked best. Have you chosen one yet? Which style?"

"I loved all three."

"Good because I've tallied the cost for each of them. Let me pull it up on my screen. Yes, here we go."

"Philip, wait. How did you do it?"

"It wasn't too hard. I figured out the price of the glass, the frame, time and labor, shipping, installation. I told you this was going to be expensive, right? Because I hope you're sitting down."

Jason laughed. "No, the images. I need to know how you put our lives inside the glass."

"Oh, that. I already explained my window-building

work. Weren't you listening? The first sample was imported, the second was carefully faceted, and the third was hand-painted—every tiny detail."

"Yes, but how . . ."

"Jason, do you really expect me to give away my secrets? Google it. And when that doesn't work, search for a better answer yourself. And when you still can't figure it out, don't worry. You don't need to know. Now, I was serious. Are you sitting down? Because here are the prices, and they aren't cheap."

Jason shook his head at Philip's nonchalant reply. He smiled, only half listening to the price list. When Philip started with the least expensive, Jason realized immediately he couldn't afford any of them. He would have to replace his mother's broken window with nothing but plain clear glass, despite a whole year of saving up. He felt a twinge of disappointment, but the adrenaline pumping through his body from finding the letter wouldn't let him dwell on it.

"What do you think? Are any of those possibilities?" Philip asked when he was done.

"I'm afraid not. I'll tell Carter to spend his Christmas money elsewhere, but I still want to pay you. Madison and I are on our way to your shop now. Philip, you gave my family the best possible gift. You've earned everything I've got and more. I'm only sorry I have so little to give you."

"Are you determined to ruin my career?" Philip sounded incredulous. "First you ask me for my secrets, and now you want to pay me? Not a chance. I will not risk my license being revoked because I let you pay me for some bits of broken glass." His tone changed. "Oh, and say hello to Madison for me. She's brilliant, isn't she? And beautiful too."

Jason glanced her way. She had both hands on the steering wheel.

"Yes, she is."

Madison didn't take her hands off the wheel to gesture, but the expression on her face made up for it. "Is he talking about me? What did he say?"

"Philip says hello."

"And you replied with 'yes, she is'? I don't think so. What did he really say?"

"I'll tell you after you spill your guts about Taliatha. And your birth mom. I can't believe you kept that from me."

Her eyes narrowed. "That's not a fair exchange!"

Jason laughed again and held the phone back up to his ear.

"Philip, we'll be there in a few minutes. We're almost . . . Philip? Philip?" He turned to Madison. "He hung up."

The yellow house stood obvious and lonely in a cornfield that had been leveled by the snowstorm the night before. Empty, soggy stalks now bent low to the ground, revealing both the house and the barn that had once been hidden from the gravel road. As they bumped along, Jason thought the barn looked smaller and less imposing. The whole landscape embraced a new open expression. Sunshine beat through the cold, melting patches of glistening snow all around them.

Madison pulled up to the house, and they climbed from the car. Noticeably missing from the porch railing was the rusty sign pointing the way to "The Window Builder."

"Oh, no. No. No." Madison said. "He can't be gone already."

Jason cocked his head and shrugged. "Maybe he took a late lunch break. We have time. Let's wait inside the barn until he gets back."

"That's not what I meant." Madison's shoulders sagged.

Jason took her by the arm. "Come on. I just talked to him. He can't be far."

He led her down the muddy path behind the

house. With the crop flattened, the pathway was less narrow and restricting. They could walk side by side.

Jason focused on stepping over damp stalks that had fallen at sharp angles in front of them, so it took him by surprise when Madison said, "See? Empty. He let me visit him twice last time. I thought you'd get the same." The disappointment in her voice was palpable.

Jason raised his eyes to the barn.

The doors stood open, but no desk sat inside. A hay-strewn interior replaced the clean, well-lit glass shop from yesterday. Horse tack hung on the walls, and one by one, six horses craned their docile heads over their stall doors to watch the approaching strangers. The horses' breath was visible in great puffs from their nostrils. Another horse, still hidden from view, whinnied.

"How . . . ?" Jason said.

"One of the many mysteries, Jason," Madison replied. "When it comes to Philip, 'how' is always asked and almost never answered. Come on."

This time, Madison led Jason forward. He trudged across the clearing in disbelief. Madison went inside and put her forehead against the muzzle of the nearest horse. In return, the horse nudged its lips against her hair and neck.

Jason stopped in the same spot he had the evening before—the place from which he had watched Madison jump into Philip's arms. It had seemed so odd, her familiarity with a common craftsman who set up shop in a barn.

Now he understood why.

He was no common craftsman. And if Philip had been there, Jason would have wanted to hug him too—at least for a moment.

But he wasn't there.

In one night, Philip had vanished. In his stead, the barn was full of horses. It was strange how out of place they seemed to Jason when it should have been the other way around.

A brash voice piped up behind him.

"Well, now, have you come to pay me to rent this space out too? I wouldn't mind the extra cash, especially right before Christmas. Shipping is so expensive."

Jason turned to face a woman who was entering the clearing from the direction of the house. Her straggly brown hair was mostly swept back, but a few wiry strands were plastered with sweat to her face. In one hand she carried a bucket. The other held a handful of feed she had pulled from her apron pocket. Chickens emerged at random from the path behind

THE WINDOW BUILDER • 53

her—clucking, necks craned—until a host of them
had swarmed at her feet, restless for their meal.

She spread the rest of the feed in rapid motions
until the chickens were happy. They pecked eagerly
wherever it fell, snow or mud. The woman stepped
over them and walked toward Jason. She seemed
careworn but sturdy.

"Did you say you rented this barn?" Jason asked.

"Yep, to that Philip-The-Window-Builder fellow.
Peculiar man. He comes through town about once
a year, never for more than two or three days. He
pays to use the barn, and he relocates the animals
himself. He even helps fix up the house. Just minor
stuff mostly."

"So that's not his house?"

"No, it's my house. I grew up there, and I raised
my own children there too. When Philip comes, he
sleeps in the barn. If he sleeps at all. I guess I don't
know. He's pretty eccentric. Maybe he only naps."

Madison gave the horse one last nuzzle before
joining the conversation.

"Do you remember me? I was asking you the
same questions not too long ago."

The woman tipped her chin and squinted her eyes.
"Yes. Yes, I believe I do. You've grown up some."

Jason waited for her to say . . . *and you look so*

pretty now . . . but she didn't. She just stepped around Madison and set the bucket down by the first horse's stall.

"I've got a lot of work to do. If you want to stay, you can help."

Jason raised his eyebrows at Madison.

"Why not?" she answered. "I'm not going back to class today."

The three of them spent the next several hours feeding, grooming, oiling, and shoveling. As the sun began to set, Jason and Madison said their good-byes, and Jason slipped the money he had planned to give Philip into the woman's apron pocket.

Christmas morning couldn't arrive soon enough.

Jason had decided to keep the letter until then and give it to his mom, under the tree with the ornament. He had shown the letter to Carter but had had a hard time explaining how he found it. Carter didn't understand what the letter meant either until Jason told him about the baby brother or sister they had almost had, and how their father had been on the way to buy flowers for their mom when the spinout happened.

"How do you know this stuff?" Carter had asked.

"Oh, you know," Jason had answered. "I saw a vision."

"No, I'm serious," Carter had replied. "I want to know how you found out about the miscarriage, the fight, the letter, and the reason dad was across town when the crash happened. Is this for real?"

"Yeah, Carter, it is," Jason had said. "And even though I want to—I really, really want to—I can't explain right now how I learned all of this." He thought of the card in his pocket, the one that said *When Carter needs my services, call me.* "I promise I'll explain someday. I'll tell you everything as soon as I can. But for now, you have to believe me."

That hadn't gone over well with Carter, and Jason suddenly had more empathy for why Madison had kept her experience to herself.

But now Christmas morning was here.

Carter had helped Jason cradle the letter and the ornament inside a bag of cotton balls before packing them down inside a cinder block. They put the cinder block inside a box and wrapped the whole thing in shiny paper. Even though Carter was still miffed, he was the one who suggested the creative packaging. They both signed their names.

Jason placed the present under the tree after his mom had gone to bed. There were no stockings this year. They had all agreed—one gift apiece. There wasn't money for more.

Jason was so excited for his mom to open their gift that he had slept less than an hour before he woke to the aroma of waffles, sausage, and hot chocolate wafting under his bedroom door. Jason inhaled slowly and reflected on those scents. They felt like a symbol of his mother's strength. Despite her personal sorrows, his mom had buried them as best she could to give Jason and Carter all she had.

Carter stuck his head out from the bottom bunk.

"Showtime," he declared.

Jason laughed. Carter might not understand Jason's secrecy, but he was still the greatest twin brother on the planet.

"Showtime," Jason agreed.

All three of them sat around the kitchen table in their pajamas, enjoying the delicious tastes of Christmas breakfast. Jason loved seeing his mom so relaxed. It was one of her only days off from both school and work. For one brief moment he worried that giving her the letter would be too much, would bring up events and emotions she might not want to feel.

Then he remembered how he felt when he discovered his father's letter above the bookcase. He knew his mother needed it.

Jason cleared his dishes from the table.

"Mom," he said. "I'm going to make your bed."

The look she gave him made him wonder why he didn't make her bed every day.

I should, he thought. *Maybe I will.*

But as soon as he entered her bedroom, he walked to the broken window instead. He lifted the cardboard away and put his hand to the cracks. Frigid air poured through. A small, palm-sized shard was missing, and again, Jason was reminded of his experience with Philip. He would never look at a piece of broken glass the same way.

Jason wished, somehow, he had been able to give his mom both the letter and the new stained-glass window. He remained there for another minute, staring motionless, feeling the freezing air seep through before he taped the cardboard back in place and actually made her bed.

The Christmas gift exchange started with his mom giving them her presents.

She gave Jason a small book about modern American architecture, but when he opened to the first chapter, he was stunned to find a note written by his Architecture Club advisor. The note confirmed payment for a field trip to Washington, DC, at the end of the school year. Jason had helped plan the trip from the beginning, thinking all along that he wouldn't be able to attend.

"Mom!" he said. "How did you . . .?"

"Nope," she said. "No *how*s this morning. You, my inquisitive child, may not know how. Just know that I love you."

Even as he hugged her, Jason realized her rule would work to his advantage.

She gave Carter a ticket to a New York Knicks game. He whooped and jumped in the air—so high that Jason worried his head might hit the ceiling.

"I figured if Jason gets to travel, you should too," she said. "I've arranged for you to go with the Gorslow family on their family vacation. It may be a long drive, but the Gorslows bought a Knicks ticket for Adam too. You'll be attending the game together."

Jason couldn't have been happier for Carter. Adam was a guard on the high school basketball team and one of Carter's best friends. Even after Carter sat down, he was still bouncing his knees in delight.

There was only one gift left under the tree.

Jason and Carter grabbed it together and made a big display of how heavy it was to carry over to their mom on the couch. They sat on the floor to watch. The anticipation was overwhelming. Jason could barely breathe.

His mother tore off the paper, opened the box, and burst out laughing.

"Oh, boys! A huge brick. You shouldn't have."

Carter chimed in. "Because you are the foundation of our lives."

But Jason couldn't speak. She had found the bag of cotton and was pulling it out of the cinder block's hollow space. She puzzled over it a moment before opening the bag and pulling out the ornament.

She looked straight at Jason, and he could sense her panic from the expression in her eyes. Now that he knew what had happened that week—that day his dad had died—Jason understood why she had hidden the ornament in a drawer. Holding it now forced in the exact emotions that had shattered her heart.

"Wait, Mom, don't cry," Jason said. He was up on his knees now, pleading. "There's more. There's more there. In the cotton balls. Open it. Then you'll understand."

She sucked in a breath, trying to hide her pain. Jason helped her. He reached over and extracted the letter and laid it on her lap.

"What is this?" she asked. Her voice sounded thick.

"Open it," Jason said.

Carter touched her arm. "You should open it, Mom."

Cautiously, she unfolded the paper. Jason saw her eyes widen in astonishment as she skimmed the words. She read the first few lines steadily, unblinking. Then her whole face changed. She covered her mouth with both hands and let out a great heaving sob. Her whole body shuddered.

She stood up. She sat down. She stood up again.

"James," she said. "Sweet James."

She clutched the letter and began to pace while she read, tears streaming freely down her face. Her skin was red and splotchy. Minutes later, she began to hiccup as she cried, her body shaking. Jason and Carter exchanged a glance. Jason had never seen his mother so uncontrolled. He hoped he had done the right thing.

He hesitated. She must have had time to read it seven times by now.

"Mom?" Jason said.

She took a deep steadying breath before turning toward them. Jason didn't know if it was the effect of the tears, but her eyes were clear and intense, like two brilliant lights set into her face.

"Where did you find this? How long have you had this?" Her strong tone took Jason by surprise. Carter looked at Jason too, hopeful for an explanation.

"I'm sorry," Jason said. "Not long. I found it, and

we just wanted to . . ." But the words wouldn't come.

"Boys," she said, her arms open. She stood like that a moment before her bottom lip trembled and the tears flowed again, unabashed. She crossed to them, dropped on her knees, and embraced them both tightly, saying, "Thank you," over and over.

Jason bit his lip hard and looked over his mom's shoulder at Carter, who was sniffing back his own tears.

"We'll get through this," said Jason. "That's what Dad always said when something went wrong. And we will."

They hugged each other for a long time, taking turns sharing little memories about past years. Their mom cried a lot, but most of those memories were happy ones, and she laughed a lot too. Finally, she flexed her cramped knees and stood up.

"What an amazing Christmas," she said. "I don't know where you boys found this letter, but it has already changed my life." She stretched again before picking up the stained glass ornament and gazing at it tenderly. She took a deep breath and hung it at the top of the tree, next to a yellow light. A moment later she nodded her head. "That seems right, doesn't it?"

Jason smiled from ear to ear.

His mother beamed. "Now, since I probably look

like a red-eyed monster . . . you don't have to nod . . . I'm going to clean up and get dressed. Maybe we could go outside for a stroll before lunch." She winked at both of them as she walked away.

Carter slugged Jason's shoulder. "However this happened—good job, Jason." He wandered toward the kitchen. "Think I'll call Adam about that Knicks game now."

Jason had just settled back onto the couch to read his new book when his mom rushed from her bedroom with a stunned expression.

"Carter!" she shouted. "Jason! I . . . I can't believe it! It's beautiful. Come quickly and see!"

Jason hurried toward her bedroom.

"What's going on?" Carter whispered.

"I have no idea," Jason muttered back.

As he passed Carter, he heard him say, "Hey, Adam, I've got to go. Call you back later." He looked as confused as Jason felt.

His mom threw open her bedroom door as Jason rushed in. The whole room blossomed in rich hues. They stared in utter stillness at a perfect full-size replica of the stained glass ornament, installed where the cracked window had been minutes earlier. Carter stopped in his tracks behind them.

Finally Carter spoke. "Dad would have liked this."

"Yes," she could only whisper. "How did you manage it?"

Jason bit his thumb knuckle for a long time before answering. "There's no telling how, Mom. There's no telling how."

*C*ARTER STARED OUT THE LIBRARY WINDOW. The semester hadn't gone at all like planned. He grabbed his books and headed out into the night.

Freezing air stabbed at his lungs. He zipped up his coat—covering his mouth and nose—and trudged through the snow toward his apartment. Syracuse University was noisier than usual at this hour. Sometimes when he headed home late he felt like he was alone on campus. But finals were almost over, and students were out in celebratory groups sharing their mutual relief before parting ways for Christmas.

He felt an arm wrap around his shoulders.

"Congratulations, man!" Jason said. "What a great end to an otherwise terrible year. Who would have thought a freshman basketball walk-on like you could become one of the big men on campus by his senior year? Unbelievable. You might actually be drafted next summer. Maybe you don't need to study so much after all."

Carter glanced at his brother. He didn't feel like celebrating anything.

Jason got the hint. He slid his arm off and jammed his hands in his pockets. They walked next to each other in silence. Carter concentrated on the sound of the snow crunching beneath his feet.

Jason broke the quiet. "How are you holding up?"

"Been better," Carter said.

"Is it your last exam tomorrow?"

"What do you think?"

"No. All right, I know it's not. Amie, then?" Jason asked.

Carter nodded without looking up. Hiding anything from his twin was useless—Jason could read him too easily. But he wasn't sure he was ready to talk about it either. *Ironic*, he thought, *for a communications major.*

"Still distant?"

Carter dropped his head lower and nodded again.

"She's been through a lot, Carter, with the fall and everything. I mean, you have too—I get that—but she must be fighting a million emotions."

"A million and one," Carter said, mumbling into his coat.

"What?"

"Nothing," he answered, more clearly this time.

Jason stopped in his tracks. Carter took a few more steps before he was willing to turn around and face him. It felt like an old-fashioned dual. There was definite tension. But instead of drawing a gun, Jason said, "I want to help. What's going on?"

Carter shifted his books from one arm to the other. "She broke it off."

Jason let out a low whistle. "When?"

"This morning. Over breakfast."

"Oh, man. I'm sorry, Carter. Any chance she'll change her mind?"

"That's the thing," Carter answered. "She could barely get the words out. I don't think Amie wants to break it off at all. She just doesn't want to be a burden." Now that his big news was out in the open he needed to tell Jason everything. "She's trying to make life easier for me. But by breaking off our engagement? That doesn't make anything easier."

"Is she still coming for Christmas? Because you know Mom will charm her into going through with the wedding."

"She already cancelled her plane ticket."

Carter watched Jason kick at the snow. "Mom will be really disappointed. She's been dying to meet her. She's spent the last week putting in ramps around the house."

"Don't you think I know that?" Carter didn't mean to sound so harsh. He took a deep breath. "Amie's mind is made up."

"Of course it is. Amie is the most determined girl I've ever met. That's why you two are so good for each other."

"Tell me about it."

"I could talk to her—give her my official Twin Seal of Approval. Seriously, I'll tell her you don't want to marry her out of duty . . . or pity. Because I know you wouldn't. I know you really want to be with her, forever."

"Listen, Jason. Not to disappoint you and Mom more, but if Amie'll let me, I think I'll stay here for Christmas again this year. She's got to understand that I'm not giving up on us. We're in this together."

Carter knew Jason would do his best to hide his regret. They had been planning visits with old friends back home plus a bunch of other family activities over the holidays. They'd made special arrangements to be sure Amie would be able to participate in everything.

Jason's face was taut for a moment before he said, "Yeah. Yeah, sure. Definitely. Get this straightened out. You two belong together. I've already written my best man's toast. We can't let it go to waste, now, can we?"

"There's one other thing," Carter said.

"Anything."

"Remember how I had the perfect gift picked out for Amie? Well, I shipped it home. I won't have time to ship it back, not this close to Christmas. I've got to find something else. And—under the circumstances—it's got to better than perfect. Maybe a really unique piece of jewelry? Something to help her see what I see, that she's beautiful inside and out. Any ideas?"

Jason took a few steps toward him, smiling. He pulled out his wallet and removed a tattered old business card.

"As a matter of fact, yes, actually. Wow. I've never been so sure of something in my entire life. You convince Amie to let you spend Christmas with her, and I'll introduce you to The Window Builder. He'll have exactly what you need."

Discussion Questions

1. How did you feel when you were first introduced to Philip, The Window Builder?

2. At what times could Jason have made different choices in the story? How might those choices have changed the outcome of the story?

3. Where did you see the theme of light throughout the book?

4. Do you relate to any of the characters? If so, how?

5. Which two characters do you think have the strongest relationship in the book? Why?

6. What do you think will happen when Carter meets The Window Builder?

About the Author

KELLY HOOSE JOHNSON grew up in flat West Texas. Influenced by a fierce sun and even fiercer storms, she played hard with her brothers and watched the night stars for hours at a time with the family dog, Panama Jack. Her brilliant parents and dedicated teachers encouraged her to try everything, supporting creativity in all forms. Many years later, she continues to dabble in variety and to thrive on new challenges, professionally and personally.

Always seeking inspiration for writing, the idea for *The Window Builder* came to Kelly in a vivid dream. She lives in the Rocky Mountains with her young family and two dogs. She still loves sun, storms, and stars.